World Of Warcraft: Shadow Wing Vol. 2

Story by: Richard A. Knaak
Art by: Jae-Hwan Kim

Layout & Lettering - Erika Terriquez
Creative Consultant - Michael Paolilli
Cover Designer - Louis Csontos
Cover Artist - Jae-Hwan Kim
Cover Art & Colors Retouch - Michael Paolilli
Cover Designer - Arnett Taylor

Editors - Troy Lewter and Paul Morrissey
Editorial Translator - Janice Kwon
Print Production Manager - Lucas Rivera
Managing Editor - Vy Nguyen
Senior Designer - Louis Csontos
Art Director - Al-Insan Lashley
Director of Sales and Manufacturing - Allyson De Simone
President and C.O.O. - John Parker
C.E.O. and Chief Creative Officer - Stu Levy

BLIZZARD ENTERTAINMENT
Senior Vice President, Creative Development - Chris Metzen
Director, Creative Development - Jeff Donais
Lead Developer, Licensed Products - Mike Hummel
Publishing Lead, Creative Development - Micky Neilson
Senior Story Developer - James Waugh
Art Director - Glenn Rane
Director, Global Business Development and Licensing - Cory Jones
Historian - Evelyn Fredericksen
Additional Development - Samwise Didier, Cameron Dayton and Tommy Newcomer and Max Thompson

gear.blizzard.com

Library of Congress Cataloging-in-Publication Data available.

This book contains material originally published by TOKYOPOP Inc.

First Blizzard Entertainment printing: March 2011
Reprinting: October 2022

ISBN: 978-1-956916-04-1

10 9 8 7 6 5 4 3 2 1

Printed in China

VOLUME TWO

NEXUS POINT

STORY BY
RICHARD A. KNAAK

ART BY
JAE-HWAN KIM

World of Warcraft

Shadow Wing

FASTER!
A WHIPPING TO ANY
FOOL WHO SLOWS
US DOWN!

Ragnok's army marches toward the Dark Portal. The death knight had been so certain of his impending triumph over his rivals, the Dragonmaw clan, that he had already prepared his followers for this next step...

That confidence had not been misplaced...

For the attack on the Dragonmaw, savage as it had been, had merely been a trial preceding a far more significant battle...

One in which Ragnok also expects to easily succeed...

But which others still hope to win instead...

WE MUST REACH THE ENCAMPMENT SOON! IT MUST BE WARNED BEFORE RAGNOK CAN UNLEASH HIS NETHER DRAGONS UPON IT!

I ONLY PRAY THAT TYRI WILL BE ALL RIGHT IN THE MEANTIME...

THESE DISTORTED EGGS... ONCE BLACK DRAGON EGGS... THEY'RE SATURATED WITH NETHER DRAGON ENERGY...
THE NETHER DRAGONS ARE DEATHWING'S ***DESCENDENTS***...
WHO IS THIS DEATHWING?!?
VALOKU!

YOU *KNOW* WHAT THIS ALL MEANS! YOU KNOW WHAT WE *TRULY* ARE! EVEN THE GREAT MATRIARCH, KARYNAKU, KNOWS NOT WHERE WE CAME FROM! YOU MUST TELL ME!

A PLAN, NO DOUBT, SET IN MOTION BY THEIR DIRE LORD, DEATHWING...

"DEATHWING, WHO SEEKS UTTER DOMINION OVER AZEROTH AT ALL COSTS... AND NO MATTER HOW MANY LIVES IT TAKES..."

DEATHWING, WHO WOULD HAVE SUCCEEDED, IF NOT FOR THOSE WHO WOULD STAND AGAINST HIM…
ESPECIALLY THE OTHER GREAT ASPECTS…

MANY HAVE PERISHED, MOST EXPENDED BY THEIR LORD IN HIS ATTEMPTS TO FULFILL HIS MAD SCHEMES...
"THEIR EGGS DESTROYED WHEREVER THEY ARE FOUND IN THE HOPES OF STAMPING OUT THEIR EVIL..."
"BUT CLEARLY DEATHWING PLANNED AHEAD, KNEW THE DANGER TO HIS KIND, AND THROUGH THE ORCS, TRANSPORTED AS MANY EGGS AS HE COULD..."
WHEN HE ENTERED THIS WORLD, I DO NOT KNOW, BUT HE CLEARLY DID. THEN, HE SECRETED THE EGGS HERE...

BUT THOUGH HE LEFT GUARDS AND LIKELY INTENDED TO RETURN... SOME OTHER ENEMY MUST HAVE APPEARED...

I KNOW THIS ANSWER, BLUE ONE. IT WAS THE GRONN--GRUUL, THE DRAGONKILLER STILL BOASTS TO ALL WHO CAN HEAR OF THESE THINGS.

WHEN THE EGGS FINALLY HATCHED, WHAT EMERGED WERE NOT BLACK DRAGONS.
"SOME WERE INCOMPLETE-- UNFORTUNATE, DEFORMED HYBRIDS THAT DIED QUICKLY."
"BUT FROM THOSE THAT THRIVED, THERE CAME SOMETHING... UNIQUE."
KRAAAAK
KRACKLE
"THE FIRST OF YOUR KIND, VALOKU--THE FIRST NETHER DRAGON!"

A BLENDING OF AZEROTH AND OUTLAND, A FANTASTIC NEW SPECIES OF DRAGON.
AND A SWIFTLY MATURING ONE! IT CAN'T HAVE BEEN THAT LONG SINCE THE LAST HATCHINGS... AND EVEN IN THE SHORT TIME I'VE KNOWN YOU, I'VE SEEN HOW YOU'VE CHANGED. YOU ARE ALREADY *QUICKER* OF WIT.
WE AGE SWIFTLY AT FIRST, THEN IT SLOWS.
I... SEE... PERHAPS IF WE CAN FIND--
BUT WE *ARE* SHORTER OF LIFE.
WE DO NOT LIVE SO LONG... OUR ENERGY FADES... I HAVE SEEN THIS WITH THOSE WHO FIRST HATCHED...
VALOKU!! TYRYGOSA!!

ZZERAKU!
WHAT IS IT?

YOUR WORD... I TRUST... *THEIRS*... WE SHALL SEE...

STOP THIS FOOLISHNESS!

HE IS EVEN NOW IN CONFERENCE WITH COMMANDER DURON IN HIS TENT.

BUT THOUGH I MIGHT TAKE YOU AT YOUR WORD, JORAD, YOU'LL CERTAINLY GO NO FARTHER UNTIL YOUR COMPANION'S ALSO BEEN ACCOUNTED FOR.

HE IS A BROKEN AND THAT IS ALL THAT MATTERS! HE *CANNOT* BE TRUSTED--

ONE BROKEN HAS FAR MORE... HONOR... THAN *ALL* THE DRAENEI!

THERE IS NO TIME FOR THIS! THE ENCAMPMENT IS IN IMMINENT DANGER!

TAKE US TO LORD TRUEBLADE AND COMMANDER DURON! THEY *NEED* TO HEAR THIS!

TELL YOUR TALE AND I'LL RELAY IT TO THE OFFICER ON DUTY! HE'LL DETERMINE WHETHER YOU REMAIN FREE, MUCH LESS SEE HIS LORDSHIP.

I TELL YOU THERE IS NO TIME FOR ALL THAT!

NO TIME FOR WHAT?

AND WHO IS THIS OUTSPOKEN PALADIN, IRULON?

And back in the mountains...

ARE YOU SURE, ZZERAKU? DID YOU TRULY SEE THAT?

YES! YES! I CHASED AWAY A PATROL COMING TOO NEAR! I FOLLOWED THEM AND THEN SAW OTHERS OF OUR KIND FAR IN THE SKY!

SLAVES! ALWAYS SLAVES TO OTHERS! WE WILL NOT TAKE THIS ANY LONGER! VALOKU WILL BE NO ONE'S SLAVE!

GO ON, ZZERAKU, TELL US MORE.

I SAW THEN THE OTHERS WHO ONCE SERVED THE DRAGONMAW CLAN-- SAVE BUT KARYNAKU, OF COURSE--FLYING AS SLAVES TO RAGNOK...

AND NO SOONER DID RAGNOK WIN, THAN THEY TURNED TO THE DIRECTION OF THE PORTAL!

THEY MOVE WITH MUCH SPEED AND KNOW THE QUICK WAYS THROUGH.

AND THIS ISN'T SO VAST A LAND... THEY'LL NOT NEED LONG TO REACH THE PORTAL...

DO YOU NOT SEE IT, ZZERAKU? THE GREAT MATRIARCH WAS NOT WITH RAGNOK'S SLAVES! THE MAGIC CHAINS OF THE DRAGONMAW CLAN'S MASTER, ZULUHED, MUST STILL TRAP HER! ZULUHED MUST LIVE...

WHAT OF IT? WHAT DO I CARE OF THEM?

YES! WE WILL DO THAT! THEN, WE WILL BE GREATEST!
NO! I HAVE A PLAN, BUT IT MEANS WE MUST FOLLOW RAGNOK!
NO! VALOKU IS RIGHT THIS TIME! WE WILL GO AFTER THE DRAGONMAW LEADER, ZULUHED! WE WILL SAVE THE MATRIARCH AND WE WILL BE MOST POWERFUL! IT IS DECIDED!
WAIT! WE CAN'T JUST--

COME, VALOKU!
STOP! COME BACK!
WAIT!
UNGH!

I WILL NOT STAY TRAPPED! I HAVE TO FOLLOW THEM!
FWOOOM!
THIS PLACE WILL NOT HOLD ME! I WON'T LET IT!
I CAN'T LET IT!

THWOOOOOOM!

YOU WILL LISTEN TO ME!

!!!

"AND EVEN THEN...WE MAY STILL ALL FAIL..."

CHAPTER TWO

UPON DEAF EARS

WHAT SAY YOU TO THIS MAN'S WARNING, IRULON?

JORAD MACE IS NOT KNOWN TO ME AS ONE WHO SPEAKS FALSELY, BUT HIS MIND HAS BEEN DISTRAUGHT AND THERE IS MUCH IN HIS PAST HE NEEDS TO MAKE AMENDS FOR.

HE SEEMS TO HAVE HIS SENSES ABOUT HIM NOW, AND YOU SAY HE IS HONEST. PERHAPS THERE IS SOMETHING TO HIS WORDS, THEN.
THE DRAGONMAW CLAN COULD NOT SO EASILY BE DEFEATED, I ASSURE YOU OF THAT... SUCH AN ARMY AS DESCRIBED COULD ONLY BE POSSIBLE IF THEY HAD BEEN.
OUR LEADERS HAVE WELCOMED THE BROKEN BACK INTO THE FOLD, BUT ONE MUST STILL TAKE INTO ACCOUNT... THEIR SENSE OF EXAGGERATION AND PRONENESS TO ERROR--
FOOL DRAENEI! WE HAVE... SEEN THIS ARMY... SEEN THE NETHER DRAGONS! WE ARE NOT MISTAKEN, NOR ARE WE THE HALF-WITS SOME LIKE YOU STILL THINK WE ARE!
VALWAR--
NO! YOU WERE... WRONG TO THINK THAT THEY WOULD LISTEN IF THIS DRAENEI HAS THEIR EAR...
I WILL WASTE... NO MORE TIME. MY PEOPLE WILL DEFEND THEMSELVES... AS ALWAYS!

VALWAR!!

LET HIM DEPART! WE HAVE NO QUARREL WITH HIM!

AS FOR YOU, JORAD MACE... THERE IS THE QUESTION OF DESERTION.

AND THE LIGHT... WHICH I HAD THOUGHT HAD FORSAKEN ME, BUT WHICH I HAD FORSAKEN INSTEAD...

I DID NOT DESERT! EVENTS ***FORCED*** MY PATH, NOT CHOICE, AND THAT PATH IN THE END STILL SERVED THE ALLIANCE!

...WILL VOUCH FOR MY DEDICATION TO THE SILVER HAND...

VALWAR! YOU ARE... BACK! WE FEARED FOR YOU WHILE YOU... WERE AMONG THE OUTSIDERS!

...HE WILL FIND THE BROKEN NO EASY PREY!

VALWAR!
WE HAVE COME... AS YOU ASKED...

YOUR REACTION IS... GRATIFYING... MY FATHER WOULD BE HONORED...

BUT THE OUTSIDERS REFUSE TO LISTEN... WE MUST MARCH BACK INTO ZANGARMARSH AND WORRY ABOUT OUR OWN... SURVIVAL...

WE ARE TO... GO?
WILL WE NOT EVEN HELP... THOSE OF OUR KIND ENSLAVED BY DRAGONMAW CLAN AND SURELY... NOW BY RAGNOK?

AND WHAT OF THE OUTSIDERS? WILL THEY TRULY NOT BE ABLE TO STAND AGAINST THE DEATH KNIGHT'S POWER?

LIKELY NOT... BUT THEY WILL WEAKEN HIM... THAT IS OUR BEST HOPE--
VALWAR! VALWAR!
THEY'VE BEEN... SIGHTED! THEY'RE NEARLY THERE!
VALWAR, WOULD WE NOT---
NO...
WE DO AS I SAID...

!!!

KRACKLE!
TWOOM!

I LEAVE THIS MATTER IN YOUR HANDS, IRULON. YOU ARE THE BEST JUDGE OF THIS MAN OF YOURS.
I MAY HAVE BEEN TOO HASTY...

JORAD MACE HAS FOUND HIS WAY TO THE LIGHT AGAIN. THAT SPEAKS VOLUMES AS TO THE TRUST WE CAN PLACE IN HIM.
BUT HIS TALE...

IT MIGHT BE BEST IF YOU RAISE THE ALERT--

NO...

TOO LATE!

THEY'RE HERE!

DESTROY THEM... SLAUGHTER THEM...

ALLIANCE OR HORDE, IT DOESN'T MATTER!
ALL WHO STAND IN MY WAY WILL FALL!

CONTROL OF THE PORTAL WILL BE MINE...

SOUND THE CALL TO BATTLE! IRULON! I MUST HEAD TO THE FRONT LINES! I LEAVE YOUR PALADINS TO YOUR ORDERS!
AS YOU SAY!
COMMANDER DURON--

THESE BEASTS ARE LIKE NONE OTHER! MERE WEAPONS WILL NOT--
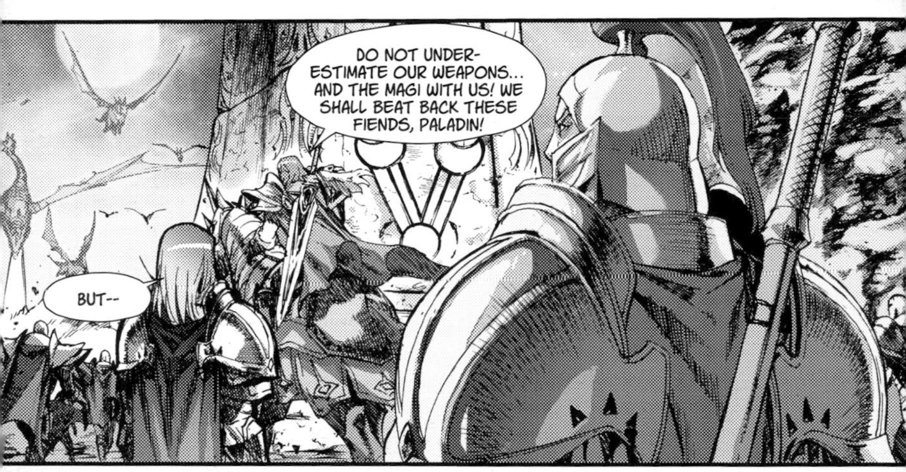
DO NOT UNDER-ESTIMATE OUR WEAPONS... AND THE MAGI WITH US! WE SHALL BEAT BACK THESE FIENDS, PALADIN!
BUT--

DURON WILL SEE TO THE ALLIANCE AS A WHOLE, JORAD.
YOUR DUTY IS NOW TO STAND WITH YOUR BROTHERS... SOMEONE! GIVE HIM A **HAMMER!**

AYE, MY LORD!

AND PRAY THE LIGHT WILL GUIDE US!

THIS IS AVAILING US LITTLE! SOMETHING MUST BE DONE!
RAGNOK! BUT HE'S TOO FAR AWAY!
AH!
IRULON!
KRACK!!

UNNF!
MY SHOULDER! THE PAIN'S GROWN STRONGER AGAIN! MUST **FIGHT** IT!

COME ON! **UP!**

THERE!

I MUST REACH HIM QUICKLY! ONLY BY TAKING HIM CAN WE HAVE A CHANCE!

EH?

FHWWAMMM!

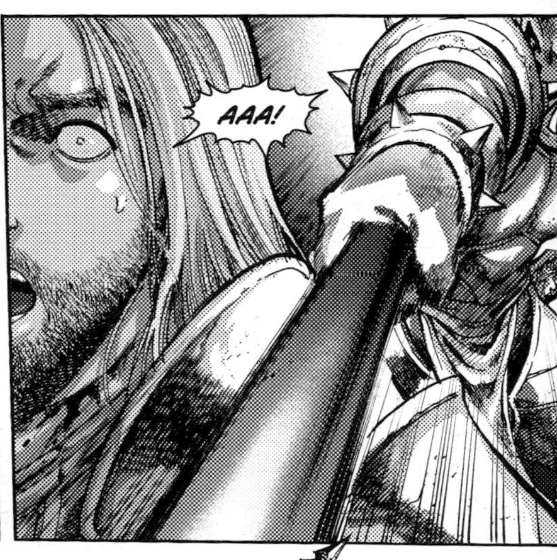

UNFH--

NO!!

STAND FAST!
SHORE UP THOSE
LINES!

THEY WILL *NOT* HAVE THE PORTAL!

PATHETIC FOOLS! BETTER TO FLEE AND HOPE TO SAVE YOUR HIDES!

NOTHING WILL KEEP THE PORTAL FROM BECOMING MINE!

NOTHING...

UNGH!

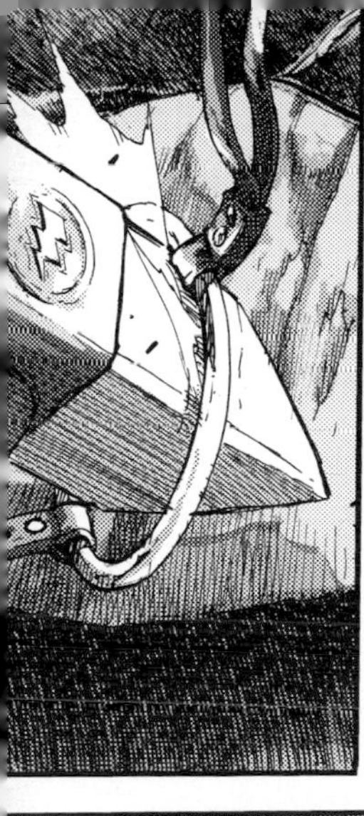

MY-- SHOULDER!
IT NEEDS HEALING DESPERATELY--BUT I CANNOT WASTE EFFORT ON MYSELF WHEN OTHERS NEED ME! THE DEATH KNIGHT MUST BE STOPPED!

YES!

UNF!
!!!

PRAISE BE!
I'VE GOT TO STOP RAGNOK--IF IT'S STILL AT ALL POSSIBLE!
WHAT'S THAT?!
THEY ARE BREAKING THROUGH!
!!!

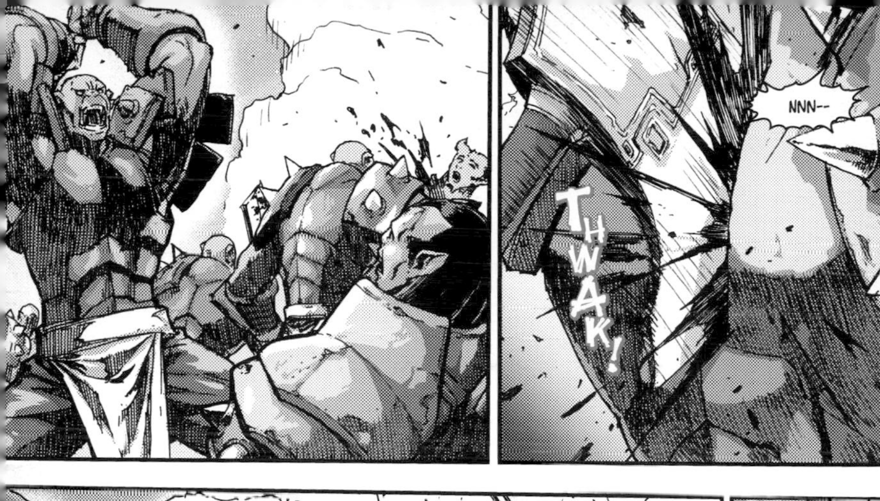
NNN--
THWAK!

AMAAN THE YOUNGER, I THOUGHT IT YOU... TAKE... MY HAND QUICKLY!

WE'VE MADE IT! BE READY!

RRRARRRH!
UNGH! THE MATRIX IS MORE INTRICATE THAN I THOUGHT, BUT... MY SPELL... MUST... WORK! IT **MUST**!
YES! IT'S... IT'S DONE!
WHAT DID YOU DO? ARE THEY FREE? ARE THEY FREE?

NO, ZZERAKU... I COULDN'T MANAGE THAT...BUT WITH GREAT EFFORT...I MANAGED TO MANIPULATE THE ARCANE ENERGIES OF THE MATRIX THAT CONTROLS THE COLLARS' OBEDIENCE SPELL...
THE MATRIX COULD NOT BE DESTROYED, BUT IT COULD BE ALTERED... NOW THEY'LL OBEY *ME* INSTEAD...
IT WAS LESS THAN I HAD HOPED FOR, BUT STILL...IT'S *SOMETHING*... AT LEAST UNTIL WE CAN TRULY *DESTROY* THE COLLARS...
SOMETHING... YES...
YOU'LL HELP US NOW! WE MUST STOP THE DEATH KNIGHT!
YES, MISTRESS...
I AM NOT YOUR MISTRESS! WHEN WE CAN, WE'LL FIND A WAY TO *FULLY FREE* YOU, I PROMISE!

NOW FOLLOW ME! HURRY!

VALWAR CAME BACK AFTER ALL!

BUT IT STILL MAY ALL BE FOR NOUGHT UNLESS THE DEATH KNIGHT IS QUICKLY DEALT WITH!

MAY THE LIGHT GUIDE ME!

RRARR!

!!!
IMPETUOUS PALADIN! ALL YOU'LL EARN YOURSELF IS A TERRIBLE DEATH!
IF DIE I MUST, THEN SO BE IT! BUT YOU'LL JOIN ME!
FOOL! THIS BODY IS ALREADY DEAD... THERE'S NOTHING YOU CAN DO!

BUT FACE YOUR DOOM...

I WILL FACE ***ALL*** THAT I MUST. AND IF I AM WORTHY, THE ***LIGHT*** WILL PROTECT ME!

AAA!

NOTHING, NOT EVEN THAT, WILL SAVE YOU ANY MORE THAN YOUR FRIENDS CAN BE SAVED FROM MY NETHER DRAGONS!

WE MUST FIND THE DEATH KNIGHT AND THE DEVICE! IT'S THE ONLY WAY TO FREE ALL THE NETHER DRAGONS AND TURN THE TIDE--

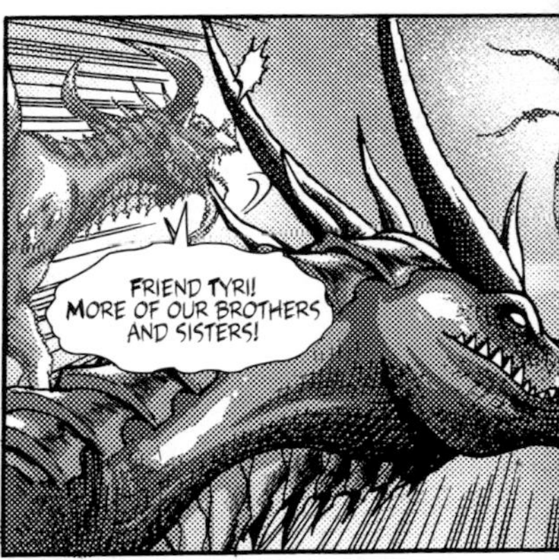

HSSS!
RRRARRH!

HSSS!

RRRARRRH!

RA--

NNNNNN!!!!

NO! YOU MUST NOT HURT OUR FRIEND! SHE WILL FREE US!

VALOKU!

UNGH!

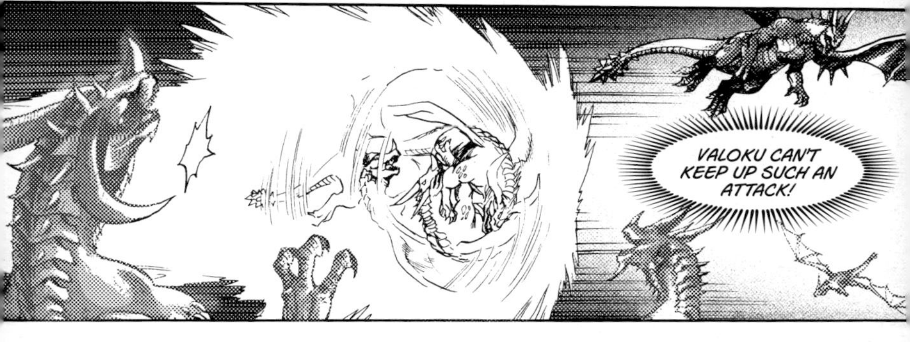
VALOKU CAN'T KEEP UP SUCH AN ATTACK!

HE'S ALREADY STARTING TO BURN AWAY!

THEY'RE CAREENING TOO CLOSE TO THE PORTAL! IF HE ISN'T CAREFUL--

ZZERAKU! **WAIT!** YOU CAN'T--

FRIEND TYRI...
ZZERAKU...
AAAA!

I WILL SAVE YOU, VALOKU!
ZZERAKU! NO! NOT SO NEAR THE PORTAL!
Z-ZZERAKU? FRIEND TYRI--

FWOOSH!!
VALOKU!
AAAAAAAA!!!

FWOOOSH!
IT'S GOING TO COLLIDE WITH THE ENERGIES OF THE PORTAL!
KRAAACKLE!
THWOOM!
KRACKLE!

ZZERAKU'S WILD SPELL--AND THE OTHER NETHER DRAGONS' UNLEASHED ENERGIES--THEY'VE ALL COMBINED TO GREATLY DAMAGE THE PORTAL!
OUTLAND IS SEALED OFF!

CHAPTER FOUR
RIFT
NO! THE PORTAL! IT CAN'T BE!

THEY'VE DESTROYED IT! KADAVAN! BLAST YOU! WHERE'VE YOU BEEN? CAN YOU--?

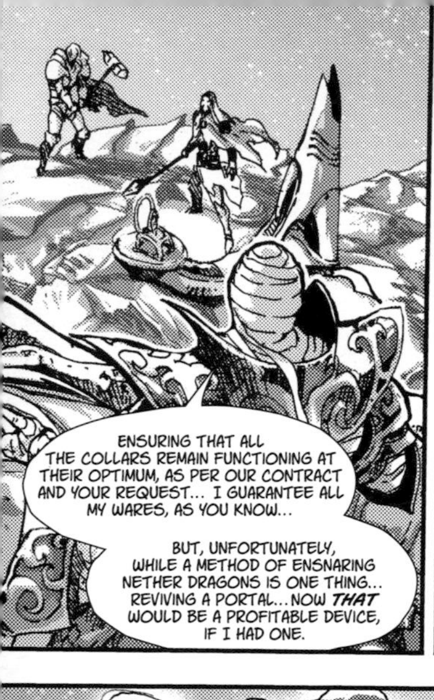
ENSURING THAT ALL THE COLLARS REMAIN FUNCTIONING AT THEIR OPTIMUM, AS PER OUR CONTRACT AND YOUR REQUEST... I GUARANTEE ALL MY WARES, AS YOU KNOW...
BUT, UNFORTUNATELY, WHILE A METHOD OF ENSNARING NETHER DRAGONS IS ONE THING... REVIVING A PORTAL...NOW *THAT* WOULD BE A PROFITABLE DEVICE, IF I HAD ONE.

CURSED DRAGON! SHE'LL PAY!

THAT MUST BE WHAT CONTROLS THE NETHER DRAGONS!

COME, DEATH KNIGHT! OUR OWN BATTLE HAS YET TO BE SETTLED!
FOOL! I'LL SETTLE IT QUICK ENOUGH...

...THEN DEAL WITH YOUR DRAGON!

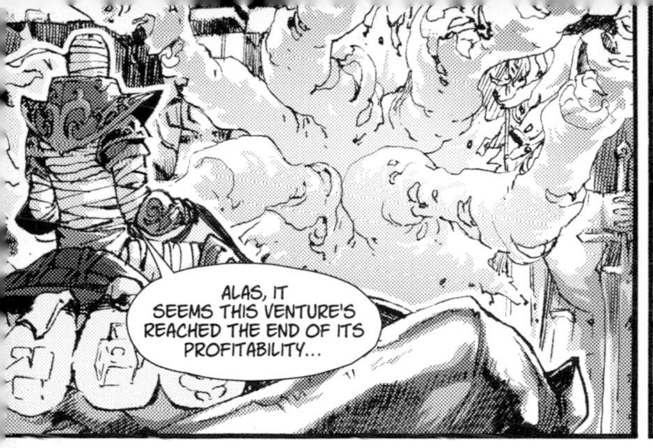
ALAS, IT SEEMS THIS VENTURE'S REACHED THE END OF ITS PROFITABILITY...

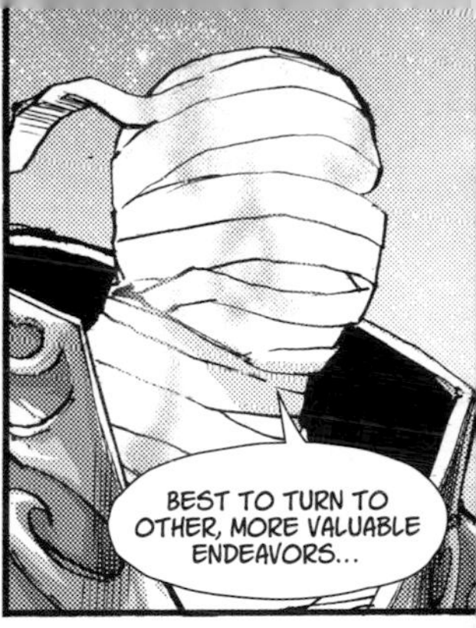
BEST TO TURN TO OTHER, MORE VALUABLE ENDEAVORS...

JORAD AND RAGNOK! AND THAT MUST BE THE DEVICE THAT CONTROLS THE OTHERS! IF WE COULD GET IT--

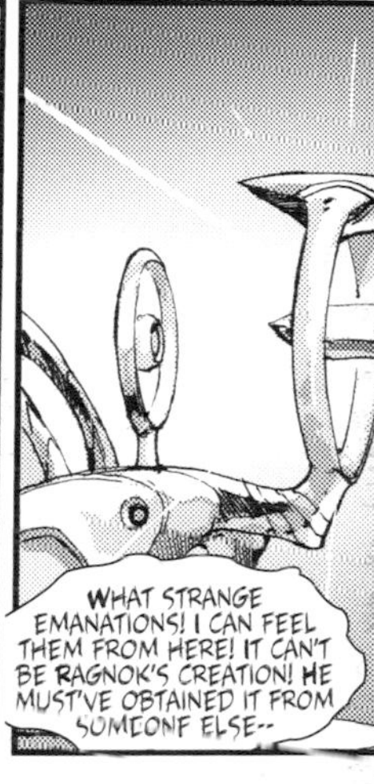
WHAT STRANGE EMANATIONS! I CAN FEEL THEM FROM HERE! IT CAN'T BE RAGNOK'S CREATION! HE MUST'VE OBTAINED IT FROM SOMEONE ELSE--

THAT KADAVAN CREATURE! HE MAY BE NEEDED IF I CANNOT DESTROY THE DEVICE...

TYRI! PERHAPS--
I PRAY SHE UNDERSTANDS!

WHY IS HE POINTING AT THAT-- THAT THING?

THAT'S NO ORC... CERTAINLY NO WARRIOR OR MAGE...FROM WHAT I CAN SENSE...COULD IT BE?

YOU'VE NO HOPE, PALADIN! GIVE IN TO YOUR DEATH, AND I MAY GRANT YOU SOME TINY MERCY!

THERE IS ALWAYS HOPE!

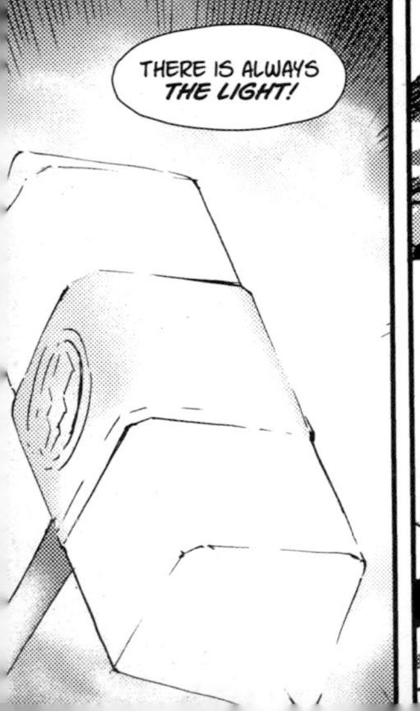
THERE IS ALWAYS THE LIGHT!

AAAAAAGGH!

UNNFF!
THWUNK!!

NOT ENOUGH! MUST TRY AGAIN!

FOOL! YOU SHOULD'VE WORRIED MORE ABOUT YOURSELF!

NOW... YOU'LL TRULY SUFFER...

A TERRIBLE SHAME! THE DEATH KNIGHT'S AMBITIONS PROMISED SO MANY POTENTIAL AVENUES OF PROFIT, SO MANY DEALS.

I WOULD HAVE A WORD WITH YOU... AND IF YOU CAN ANSWER **RIGHT,** I **MAY** LET YOU LIVE!

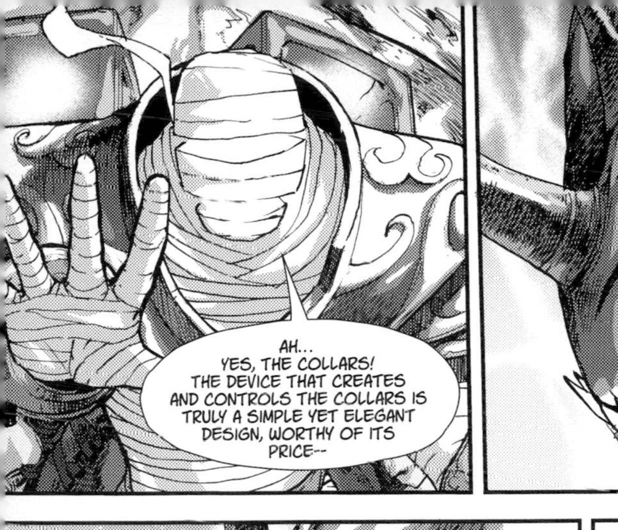
AH...
YES, THE COLLARS!
THE DEVICE THAT CREATES
AND CONTROLS THE COLLARS IS
TRULY A SIMPLE YET ELEGANT
DESIGN, WORTHY OF ITS
PRICE--

TELL--
ME--HOW--TO
STOP IT!

TRULY,
MASTERY OF THE
DEVICE IS EASY, REQUIRING THE
UNDERSTANDING OF A FEW TWISTS
AND TURNS OF ITS COMPONENTS AND
THE RIGHT ADJUSTING OF ITS
ENERGIES.
ONCE THE DEVICE IS
RETRIEVED FROM THE DEATH
KNIGHT, IT WOULD TAKE BUT
SECONDS FOR ME TO SHOW YOU
HOW TO MANIPULATE IT.

GOOD! THEN
ALL WE NEED TO DO IS
GET YOU BACK TO THE
DEATH KNIGHT!

THIS WILL GO
FASTER IF I TAKE
YOU MYSELF.
!!!

UNNNF!!

YOU RESIST MY POWER! HOW CAN THIS BE?

IT IS THE *LIGHT*--THE LIGHT IS WITH ME!

AND AGAINST IT, ALL YOUR POWER IS AS *NOTHING!*

THWAACK!

NO!

AAAA!!!

THWAK!!!

HISSSS!
RRRRAR!
RRRRAR!

WHAT IS IT?
WHAT'S HAPPENING?

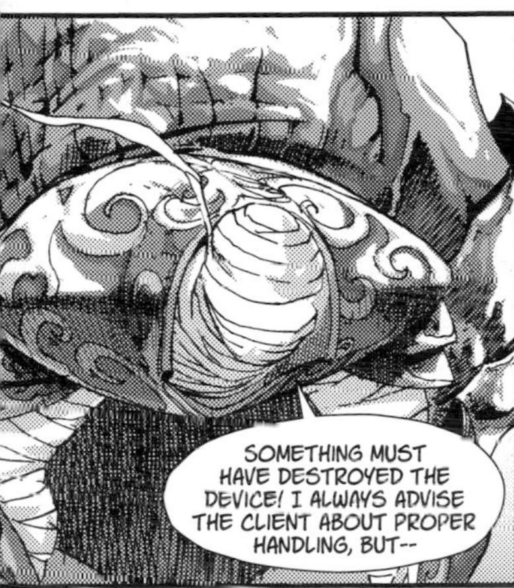
SOMETHING MUST HAVE DESTROYED THE DEVICE! I ALWAYS ADVISE THE CLIENT ABOUT PROPER HANDLING, BUT--

ENOUGH! JUST TELL ME HOW TO RIGHT THIS!

ALAS... THERE'S NOTHING TO BE DONE IF THE DEVICE IS RUINED... NOTHING AT ALL...

THE DEVICE! FOOL! WITHOUT IT, THE NETHER DRAGONS CANNOT BE CONTROLLED!

BUT YOUR VICTORY IS SHORT-LIVED! YOUR LIGHT IS TOO WEAK TO SAVE YOU FROM THE SPELL OF DECAY MY TOUCH HAS GRANTED YOU! I WILL GO ON, REGAIN CONTROL OF THE BEASTS--
NO... DEATH KNIGHT...

THIS MUST END HERE... *NOW*... AT... AT *WHATEVER*... COST!

YOUR WILL IS TOO WEAK! YOUR HOLY TRICKS WILL AVAIL YOU NOTHING THIS TIME, AND WITHOUT THEM, YOU ARE NOTHING!

WITH... OR WITHOUT THE LIGHT... I AM... AND WILL ALWAYS... BE... A PALADIN OF THE SILVER HAND...

AND THAT IS WHY YOU WILL... NOT SUCCEED...
AS FOR... FOR THE LIGHT... IT IS NO LITTLE TRICK... THE LIGHT IS THE TRUTH...
Jorad focuses inward, seeking the Light as never before and willing to make whatever sacrifice necessary...
BEFORE THE LIGHT, YOU ARE IN TRUTH NOTHING BUT A CORPSE TOO LONG LEFT UNBURIED... A FOUL SPIRIT LONG OVERDUE TO BE CAST OUT...
The strain is terrible, yet also wonderful. He knows that the price is worth it.
NO MERE MORTAL WEAPON CAN HARM ME! NO PALADIN HAS THE STRENGTH TO DESTROY ME!
More than ever, in this moment, Jorad Mace and the Light are one.
IT IS NEITHER MY HAMMER NOR I WHO WILL BE THE FORCE BEHIND YOUR DESTRUCTION, DEATH KNIGHT! WE ARE BUT THE TOOLS...
JUDGMENT HAS BEEN MADE UPON YOU NOT BY US...

BUT BY THE LIGHT!
TWHHOOM!
AND AS ONE, THEY ARE UNSTOPPABLE!

AAAAAAAAAAAAAAA!!!!!

AAAAAAA...

IT'S DONE! WITHOUT THE BODY, HIS ACCURSED SPIRIT HAS NO HOLD HERE!

I'LL MAKE YOU A NEW DEAL! GIVE ME ***ANOTHER*** DEVICE, AND ***YOU'LL*** HAVE YOUR FREEDOM, TOO!
WHILE I AM ALWAYS EAGER FOR A GOOD DEAL, I FEAR THAT I'VE NOTHING TO OFFER IN THIS CASE.

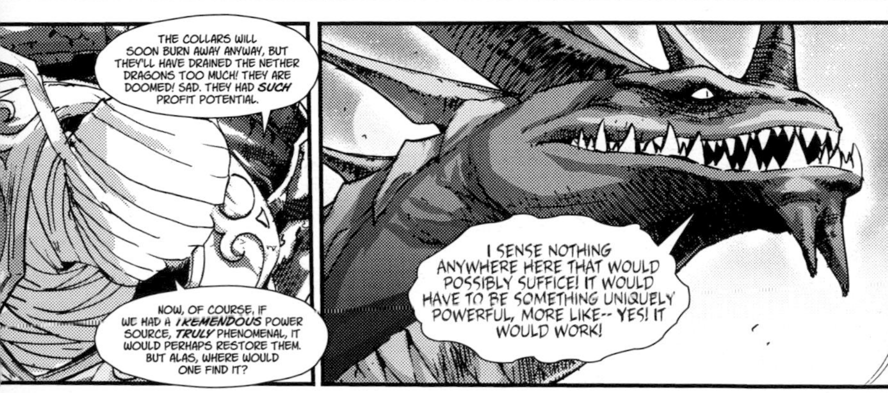
THE COLLARS WILL SOON BURN AWAY ANYWAY, BUT THEY'LL HAVE DRAINED THE NETHER DRAGONS TOO MUCH! THEY ARE DOOMED! SAD. THEY HAD ***SUCH*** PROFIT POTENTIAL.
NOW, OF COURSE, IF WE HAD A ***TREMENDOUS*** POWER SOURCE, ***TRULY*** PHENOMENAL, IT WOULD PERHAPS RESTORE THEM. BUT ALAS, WHERE WOULD ONE FIND IT?
I SENSE NOTHING ANYWHERE HERE THAT WOULD POSSIBLY SUFFICE! IT WOULD HAVE TO BE SOMETHING UNIQUELY POWERFUL, MORE LIKE-- YES! IT WOULD WORK!

BUT TO--TO REACH THAT, WE NEED THE DARK PORTAL... AND IT'S NOT WORKING! THERE'S NO OTHER PORTAL AVAILABLE--

UNLESS...

ZZERAKU! QUICKLY!

ZZERAKU! I KNOW A PLACE WHERE **ALL** YOUR KIND CAN BE RESTORED BEFORE IT'S TOO LATE! BUT I'LL NEED YOU TO GATHER THEM DESPITE THEIR AGONY!

WHERE IS THIS... MIRACULOUS PLACE?

ON AZEROTH...

BUT HOW DO WE--?

UNNGH!

IF I CAN JUST GET LOW ENOUGH...

!!!

THWACK!

JORAD MACE! I SAW YOU ABOVE, SEEKING THE MASTER OF THE NETHER DRAGONS!

THAT YOU ARE HERE GIVES ME HOPE THAT YOU WERE VICTORIOUS!

'TIS TRUE, THE DEATH KNIGHT WHO LED THIS IS NO MORE, BUT WHAT IS HAPPENING TO THE NETHER DRAGONS WAS NOT INTENDED BY ME!

WHAT OF IT? WE ARE BETTER RID OF THE BEASTS! MY CONCERN IS FOR THE ALLIANCE AND SOMEHOW OPENING THE PORTAL AGAIN--

EH?

BY THE LIGHT!

AZEROTH IS THEIR ONLY HOPE. AND THAT ONLY HOPE LIES IN A DIMENSIONAL RIFT.
OPENING ONE IS ALMOST IMPOSSIBLE... WITHOUT RISK! BUT I HAVE TO!
KRAACKLE
KRAACKLE
KRAACKLE
THE COLLARS ARE DISSIPATING, BUT THE STRAIN HAS ALL BUT BURNED THE NETHER DRAGONS UP! THEY'LL SIMPLY FADE AWAY...
THE RIFT MUST OPEN! I WILL NOT FAIL THEM!

KRACKL
KRACKLE
KRACKL
IT'S OPENING, BUT WILL IT HOLD?! NEVER-NEVER USED SO MUCH POWER!

FWOOOOM!!!

ZZERAKU!! I DON'T KNOW HOW LONG I CAN HOLD IT TOGETHER! EVERYONE MUST FOLLOW ME THROUGH!

TO WHAT?! WHAT DO YOU PLAN?!

TO SAVE YOU!! HURRY!

RRRAAAA

WE HAVE TO FLY **FASTER!** THE STRAIN FROM THE COLLARS IS TOO MUCH! THEY CAN'T HOLD THEMSELVES TOGETHER ANY LONGER!!!

AND EVEN THEN, I COULD BE WRONG, BUT I HAVE NO CHOICE. THERE'S ONLY **ONE** PLACE THAT MIGHT SAVE THEM... ONE PLACE...
THE NEXUS...

CHAPTER FIVE

NEXUS

WE-WE'VE DONE IT! WE'RE TH-THROUGH TO NORTHREND!

THERE! THAT WAY! THE-THE ENERGIES OF THE NEXUS WILL REJUVENATE YOU!
FOLLOW-FOLLOW ME...
HEAR ME... QUICKLY...

THERE... THERE IT IS...
THE NEXUS!

ITS ENERGIES WILL BE Y-YOUR SALVATION! ALL YOU SHOULD HAVE TO DO--
?!

ZZERAKU! YOU AND THE OTHERS *MUST* KEEP UP!
W-WE ARE GROWING WEAKER! IS THIS-- IS THIS WHAT WILL SAVE US? WHAT IS THIS PLACE?

YES! THIS IS THE SANCTUM OF MY LORD, MALYGOS--LORD OF THE BLUE DRAGONFLIGHT AND MASTER OF ARCANE MAGIC!
HE WILL HELP US?

NO... HE IS LOST IN MADNESS AND DOES NOT EVEN STIR THESE DAYS! HE CAN'T AID US, BUT THE POWERFUL ENERGIES OF THE NEXUS CAN! I SWEAR!
I FEEL... I FEEL IT... THE *POWER*... YES, THIS IS IT!

COME! THIS IS OUR HOPE!
ZZERAKU--

YES!
DRAW FROM IT!
FEED FROM IT!

IT'S WORKING--
AND JUST IN TIME!

THE NEXUS IS
COMPLETELY
REVITALIZING THEM!

THEY'RE STILL
ABSORBING
POWER...

ZZERAKU! CALL THEM BACK! THEY'VE FULLY RECUPERATED!
NO...
ZZERAKU! LISTEN! YOU DON'T KNOW WHAT WILL HAPPEN--
YES...I DO... WE WILL GROW STRONGER YET...
STRONG ENOUGH SO NO ONE WILL EVER CONTROL US AGAIN! NOT EVEN YOU AND YOUR MASTER!

WHAT ARE YOU SAYING?! ZZERAKU, I ONLY SEEK TO HELP--
NO ONE HELPS US! ALL WANT TO *USE* US!
BUT WE ARE STRONG NOW! WE WILL BE *MASTERS*! THIS WORLD, THIS AZEROTH, WILL BE OUR RIGHTFUL DOMAIN!

WE WILL BE WHAT WE WERE BORN TO BE...

NO, ZZERAKU! THAT'S ALL WRONG! YOU DON'T WANT TO FOLLOW DEATHWING'S PATH! THE NETHER DRAGONS ARE NOT LIKE THE BLACK DRAGONS!

WE HAVE LISTENED TO YOU ENOUGH.

AAAAAAA!

N-NO, ZZERAKU! I-IT DOESN'T HAVE TO BE-BE THIS WAY! YOU ARE NOT BOUND TO THIS DARK PATH! Y-YOU CAN BECOME SOMETHING FAR B-BETTER!

LIES! IF WE ARE NOT MASTERS, WE CAN ONLY BE CONTROLLED!
AND WE WILL NOT BE CONTROLLED!
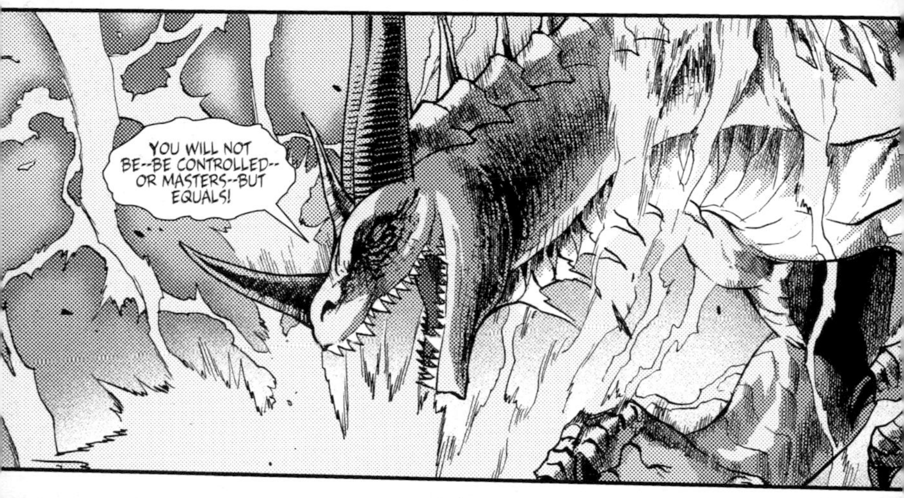
YOU WILL NOT BE--BE CONTROLLED-- OR MASTERS--BUT EQUALS!

EQUALS?

CEASE!

ARYGOS!

TYRYGOSA! AND WHAT ARE THESE--THESE MONSTROSITIES?

LEAVE...OR ELSE.

YOU FOUL--CREATURES--DARE NOT ONLY INVADE THE SANCTUM OF MY FATHER, BUT ALSO SEEK TO SLAY ONE OF OUR OWN? AND THEN YOU THREATEN *ME*?

SURRENDER IMMEDIATELY, AND I SHALL STILL BE MERCIFUL! HESITATE--AND YOU WILL ALL PAY THE ULTIMATE PRICE!

SURRENDER? NO!

A-ARYGOS!
ZZERAKU! N-NO!
D-DON'T--

HISSSSS
RRRRARR

RRRROARR
RRRAR

HISSSSS

FWOOSH
ZZZZKKKK
THWOOOM

THERE REMAINS ONLY ONE OTHER HOPE...

"BUT WILL HE HEAR ME ANY MORE THAN MALYGOS WOULD HAVE?"

KALEC! I-I'M NEAR THE NEXUS! YOU HAVE TO COME--

TYRI! I CAN'T UNDERSTAND YOU! THE LINK IS SO WEAK--

I...I NEED YOUR HELP! I CANNOT EXPLAIN, SAVE THAT THE NEXUS IS IN DANGER!
WHAT DID YOU SAY? SOMETHING ABOUT THE NEXUS?
TYRI?! TYRI?! I CAN'T SENSE YOU ANY MORE!
KALEC?! KALEC?!

I...I COULDN'T MAINTAIN THE LINK LONG ENOUGH... HE DOESN'T KNOW WHAT I WANT... HE WON'T KNOW TO COME HERE...

THERE'S NO ONE ELSE TO TURN TO...

IT FALLS TO ME... I HAVE TO MAKE ZZERAKU SEE REASON...AND EXPLAIN TO ARYGOS...

RRRROOOARRR

HISSSSSS

Fwissssss
THWWWWOOM!!

ZZERAKU! FOR THE LAST TIME, PLEASE LISTEN TO ME! THIS CAN'T GO ON!

AND IT WILL NOT... THEY CANNOT STAND AGAINST US ANY LONGER... SEE!

WE ARE TOO POWERFUL...AND WITH THE NEXUS, WE WILL GROW *MORE* POWERFUL!

ZZERAKU, THIS PATH WILL ONLY LEAD TO DESTRUCTION! YOU AND YOUR KIND ARE NOT BLACK DRAGONS! YOU ARE SO MUCH MORE AND CAN *BE* SO MUCH MORE, BUT--

FWOOOM!!!

NO MORE TALK!

UNNNGH!

WE ARE THE STRONGEST HERE NOW! WE COMMAND THIS PLACE! YOUR KIND SHALL RULE NO LONGER!

WE WILL NOT RETURN TO OUTLAND! AZEROTH WILL BE OUR HOME!

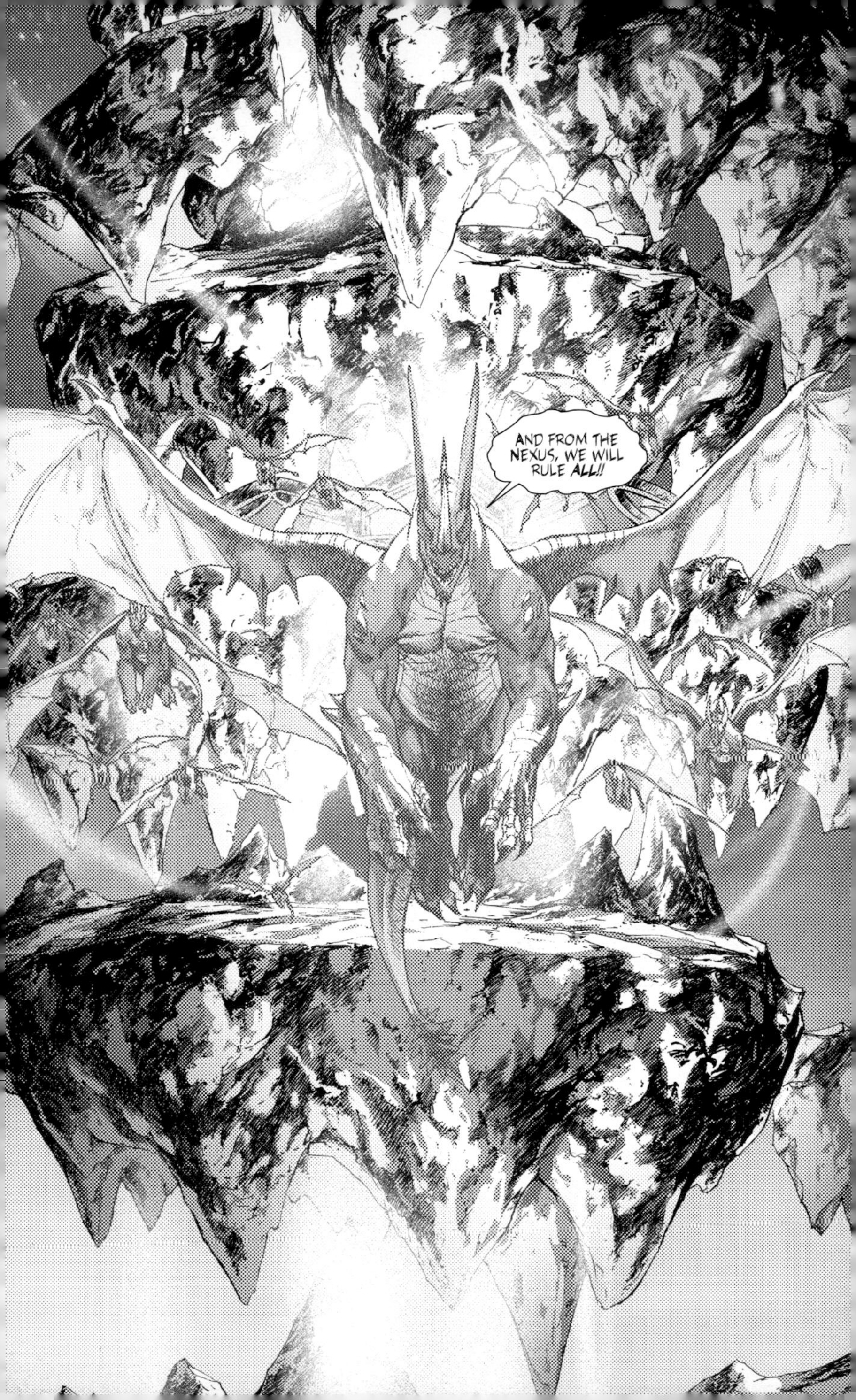
AND FROM THE NEXUS, WE WILL RULE ALL!!

CHAPTER SIX

LORD OF THE NEXUS

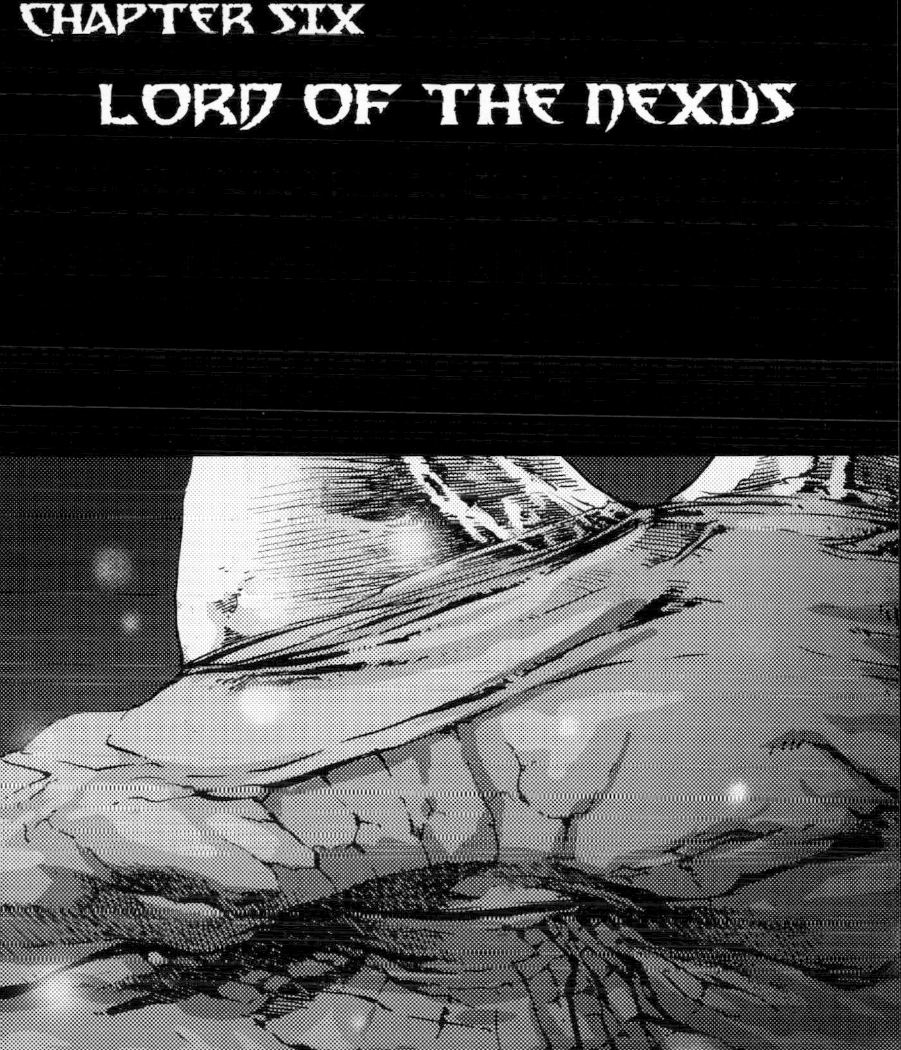

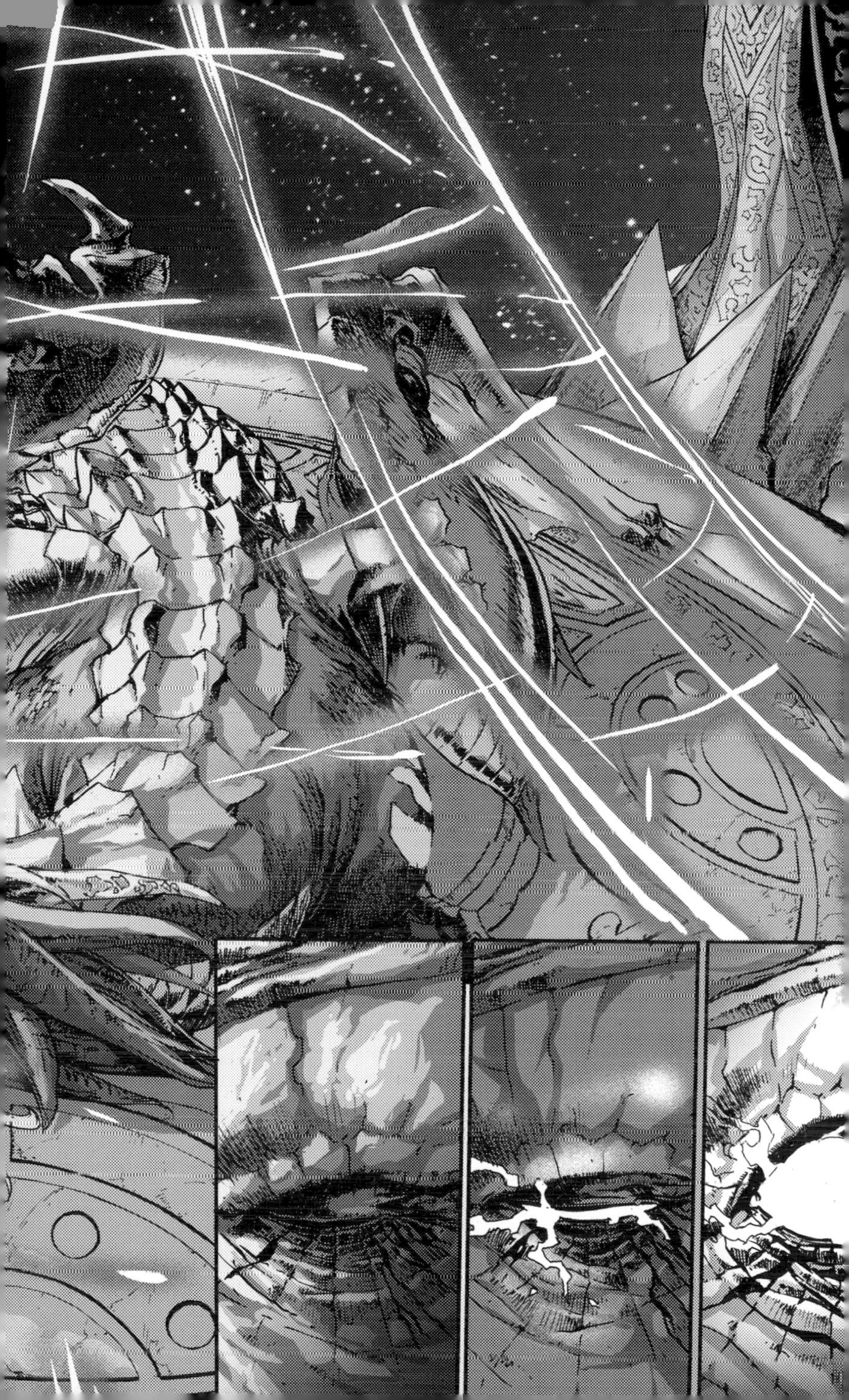

THIS WILL ONLY LEAD TO CATASTROPHE, ZZERAKU! AZEROTH WILL RISE AGAINST YOU! THAT ISN'T WHAT YOU WANT!

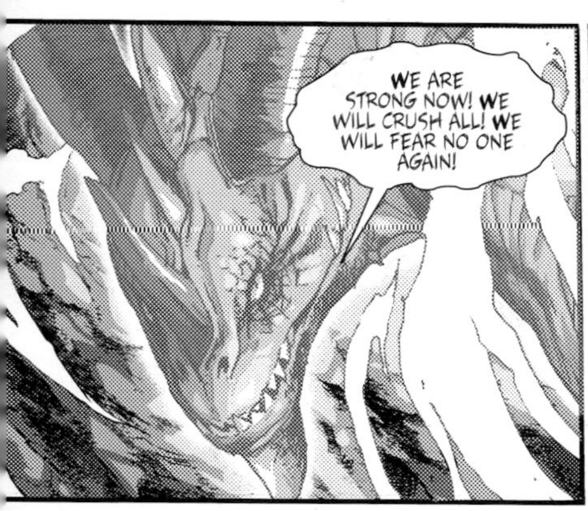

FWOOOOM!
KRAKL
KRAKL
AAAAAAAAAAAAAAAAAAAAA!
KRAKL

OH, ZZERAKU! OH, NO!

YOU DID THIS! YOU TRICKED ZZERAKU! YOU HURT HIM!

NO! LISTEN BEFORE IT'S TOO LATE! I WANT TO SAVE YOU! HE STIRS! MALYGOS STIRS! YOU DON'T UNDERSTAND WHAT THAT MEANS! HE'S--

KRAKL
WHO...DARES... DEFILE...THE NEXUS?!?
KRAKL
KRAKL

THE NEXUS IS OURS! *OURS!*

RRRRRAAAAR!

HSSSS!

HSSSS!

FWSSSST!
ZZZT
THWWWOOM!
HSSSS!

THIS IS...WRONG! ALL...WRONG!
LIAR! THIS WAS A TRAP!
THWWOOSH!

ZZZZAKK!
FFFWSSSTT!
WE ARE TOO STRONG! WE ARE MOST POWERFUL! YOU WILL ALL FALL TO US!

FWSSST!
ZZTT
FWSSSST!
!!!
I-IT'S NO USE! I-I'VE FAILED THEM!

FATHER!
FATHER!

THE NEXUS...
MY NEXUS...

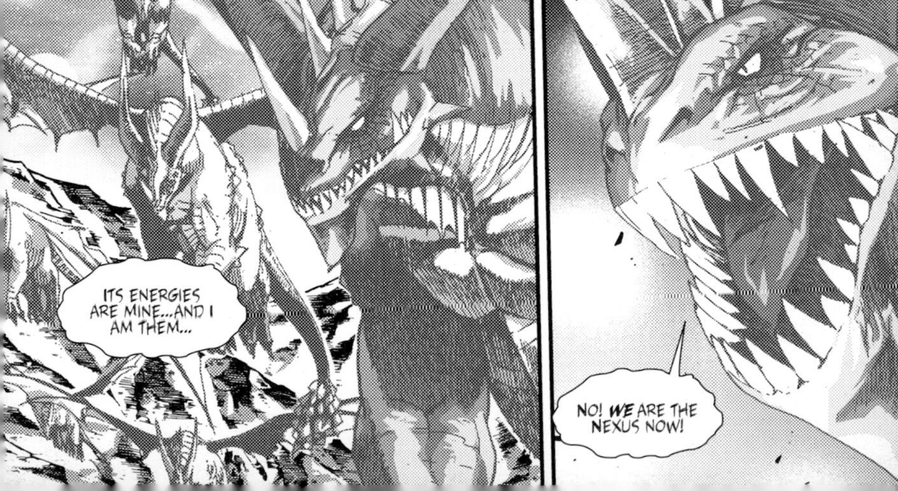

WE...ARE POWER, ***ARCANE MAGIC...***

AND I AM LORD OF ALL THAT IS ARCANE... I... AM MAGIC.

CAN'T...
FEND THEM OFF...
CAN'T--

ZZZZTT

ZZZZTTT

RARRRRRRGH!!

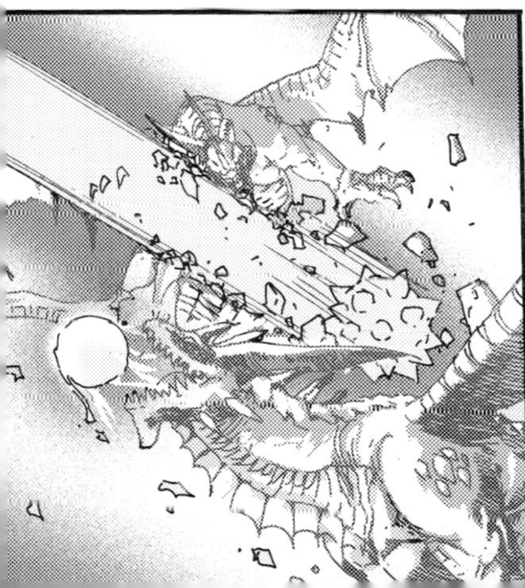

TZZZZAK
FWWWOOOOOM!!!
FWZZT!
K-KALECGOS?

PRAISE BE THAT YOU CAME! I THOUGHT MY MESSAGE DIDN'T GET THROUGH.
I WAS AFRAID THAT I WAS ALREADY TOO LATE! I'M SORRY I COULDN'T UNDERSTAND ALL THAT YOU SAID!
YOU MENTIONED THE NEXUS, BUT I NEVER THOUGHT--
IT JUST BARELY-- WHAT'S HAPPENING?!
NO! THE NETHER DRAGONS!
KALEC! WE MUST STOP THEM! THEY DON'T KNOW WHAT THEY'RE--

But Tyri realizes it is already too late...
"We are the Nexus," the nether dragons had proclaimed, not truly understanding what that might mean to the mad Malygos.
For the Nexus is the ultimate repository of arcane energies, and Malygos, even in his insanity, is still lord of arcane magic.
If the nether dragons are indeed the Nexus, by the insane Dragon Aspect's notion, they are also a part of HIMSELF...

And thus, the lord of arcane magic now returns them to where they BELONG...

I DON'T BELIEVE IT! H-HE'S ABSORBING THEIR ENERGY! THEIR VERY ESSENCE! I MUST--

NO! THERE'S NO TELLING HIS STATE OF MIND! BESIDES, IT'S ALREADY OVER!

OVER...

COULD IT BE...NO MORE?

TYRI! WHERE ARE YOU GOING?
THIS--THIS IS NOT HOW IT SHOULD HAVE ENDED FOR ZZERAKU AND HIS KIND! IT WASN'T THEIR FAULT! THEY HAD NO GUIDANCE!
I INTEND TO CHANGE THAT.

I *WILL* FIND MY WAY BACK TO OUTLAND...AND TO THOSE WHO I MIGHT STILL BE ABLE TO HELP.

I SWORE TO ANVEENA I WOULD ALWAYS PROTECT HER AND SO I NEED TO RETURN QUICKLY. BUT KNOWING HER AS I DO, I THINK SHE WOULD *INSIST* THAT I HELP YOU RETURN FIRST.

HMM, NO RETURN RIDE THERE... NO MATTER. THE PROFIT POTENTIAL FOR THAT TERRITORY HAS PLAYED ITSELF OUT, I THINK...

AND THAT HARDLY SEEMS A PLACE TO FIND AN EAGER CUSTOMER...

STILL... SOMEWHERE IN THIS NEW WORLD THERE SHOULD BE PLENTY EAGER TO SAMPLE THE WARES I CAN OFFER THEM...
ALL THEY'LL HAVE TO DO IS BE WILLING TO PAY THE *PRICE*...

And in Outland, the battle has ended in hard-fought victory.
The Alliance and Horde now seek to clear away the dead as magi from both sides move to strengthen a recently-revived Dark Portal.

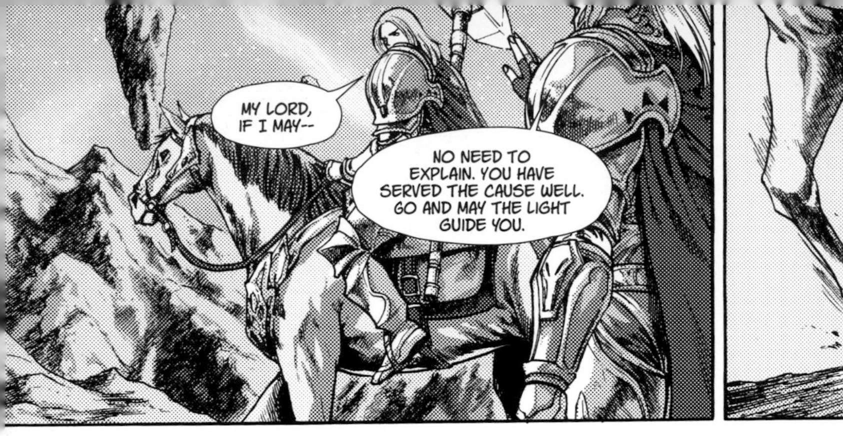
MY LORD, IF I MAY--
NO NEED TO EXPLAIN. YOU HAVE SERVED THE CAUSE WELL. GO AND MAY THE LIGHT GUIDE YOU.

TYRI! WHAT HAPPENED? THE NETHER DRAGONS--
ZZERAKU AND THE OTHERS... ARE NO MORE. LEAVE IT AT THAT.

I AM SORRY! I KNOW YOU TRIED TO HELP THEM.
IF I HAD ONLY ENCOUNTERED ZZERAKU AND HIS KIND SOONER. AND IF MY MIND HAD NOT BEEN DWELLING SO MUCH ON PAST HEADSTRONG CHOICES THAT NEARLY KILLED NOT JUST MYSELF, BUT YOU AND THE OTHERS...
AND, YES, IF NOT ALSO FOR KALEC'S REJECTION OF OUR ORDAINED BONDING BECAUSE OF HIS LOVE FOR ANVEENA... THIS MIGHT'VE ENDED DIFFERENT...

INSTEAD, NOT ONLY DID THEY PERISH, BUT YOU AND I NEARLY DID AS WELL.
IT IS HARD TO EXORCISE THE GHOSTS OF OUR PAST. I KNOW. YET, I'M SURE NO ONE COULD HAVE DONE MORE FOR THE NETHER DRAGONS THAN YOU DID, TYRI!

THANK YOU FOR SAYING SO. I'VE UNDERESTIMATED YOU, JORAD MACE.
NO. YOU'VE UNDERESTIMATED YOURSELF.

PERHAPS. NEVER MIND. I'VE SAID TOO MUCH. NOW IT'S TIME I SIMPLY SAID... FAREWELL.
YOU-- WHERE ARE YOU GOING?

LIKELY BEYOND THE MOUNTAINS. IT'S ONLY A SUSPICION... ONLY A HOPE...

IT MAY BE THAT WE WILL SEE ONE ANOTHER AGAIN. BUT KNOW THAT I WILL ALWAYS CALL YOU FRIEND, JORAD... AND BE GRATEFUL TO HAVE KNOWN YOU...
AND I, YOU. AND WE WILL MEET AGAIN, I SWEAR...
FAREWELL, TYRYGOSA. GOOD LUCK WITH WHATEVER IT IS YOU SEEK...

I SEEK TO CHANGE THE LEGACY POOR ZZERAKU THOUGHT WAS THE NETHER DRAGONS' DESTINY.
I HOPE TO BE ABLE TO SALVAGE HIS KIND'S FUTURE!

"EVEN IF I COULDN'T SAVE EITHER VALOKU OR HIM..."

WRONG... ZZERAKU WAS WRONG... TYRI WAS FRIEND... FRIEND TO ALL NETHER DRAGONS... TRIED TO TEACH US TO BE SOMETHING--SOMETHING MORE--AND I DID NOT LISTEN...

ZZERAKU... YOU ARE A FOOL! SHE-- SHE DID TRY TO SAVE ME-- ALL OF US!

THE OTHERS ARE GONE. ZZERAKU IS STILL STRONG...BUT NOT ENOUGH FOR THE GREAT BLUE ONE.
I MUST FIND FRIEND TYRI... SHE WILL TELL ME WHAT I MUST DO... YES, SHE WILL--

HAVE NO FEAR. YOUR FUTURE IS ALREADY PLANNED.
WHO DARES?

FOOLISH CREATURE! YOU DARE-- WHAT *HAPPENS*? WHAT IS THIS?
SOMETHING THE MISTRESS COMMANDED I BRING. THOUGH HOW SHE KNEW I'D FIND SUCH A CATCH IS HER SECRET...

AAAAAAA!!!!
BUT THEN, SHE HAS MANY SECRETS... INCLUDING ONE FOR WHICH YOU'LL PROVE QUITE INVALUABLE.

ONCE WE RETURN WITH YOU TO GRIM BATOL...*
*FOR MORE DETAILS ON THIS, SEE THE NOVEL, *NIGHT OF THE DRAGON*...

Epilogue

Outland: Some weeks after the Alliance and Horde, now rid of the death knight's fel orcs, resume their struggle against the Burning Legion.

And well aware that if what Tyri seeks DOES exist, she will find it.
The hope for a future for the nether dragons. A future that proves they are more than a shadow of Deathwing's evil.
A future which Tyri intends to nurture as best she can... and which in turn...
May nurture her future as well...
The End

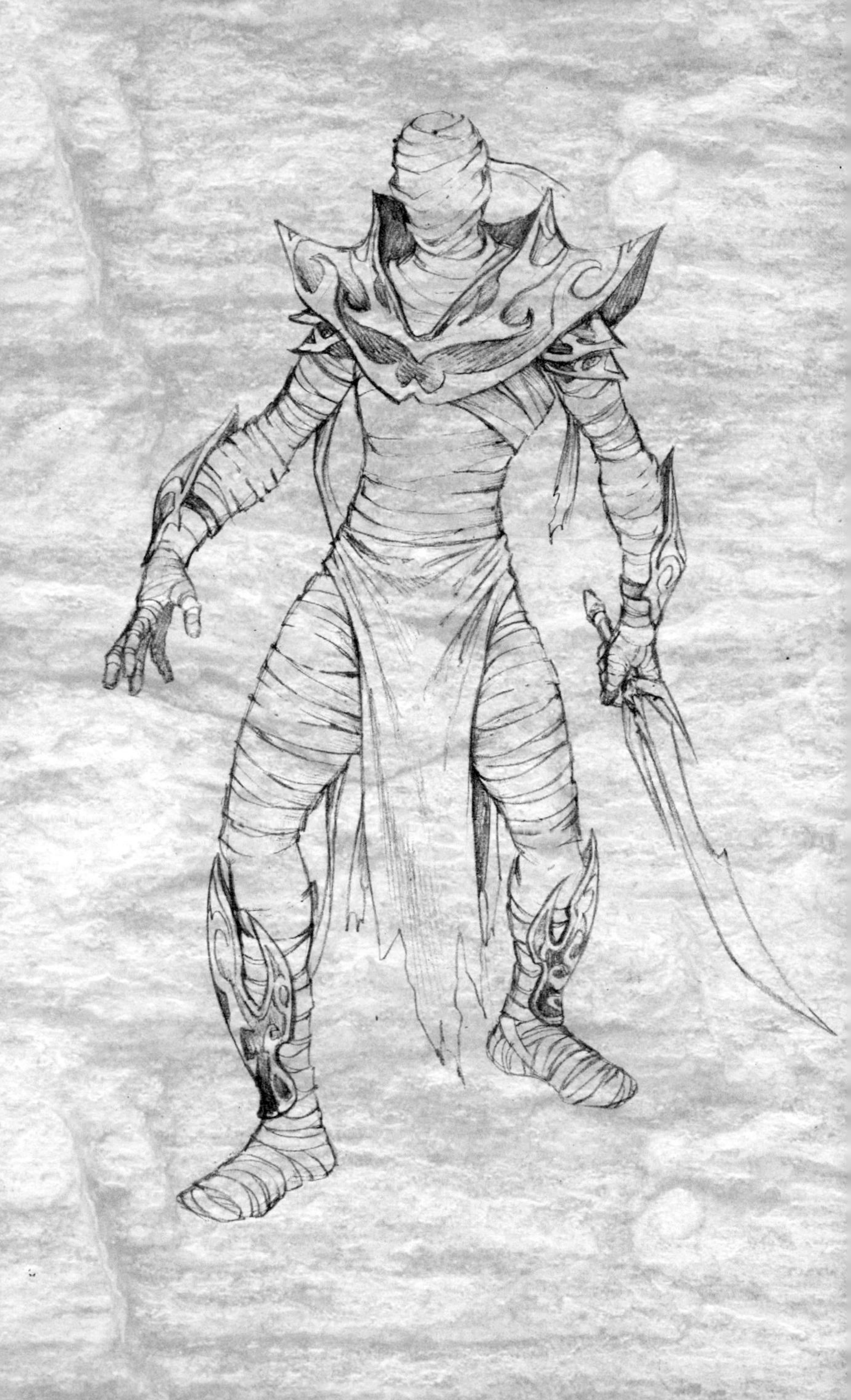

SHADOW WING SPECIAL THANKS

We hope you enjoyed *Nexus Point*, the thrilling volume two finale to *World of Warcraft: Shadow Wing*! On behalf of Blizzard Entertainment, we want to thank you for supporting this series!

Many thanks goes to the dynamic duo of *World of Warcraft* manga, Richard A. Knaack and Jae-Hwan Kim for weaving awesome stories in Azeroth for five years straight. You two should TOTALLY form your own guild now...!

This book represents not just an end to the series, but the end of three years of thrilling *World of Warcraft* manga. It has been a rollercoaster ride of late-night art revisions, last-minute script tweaks, and races to the printer finish line, but we have somehow always prevailed in the face of seemingly insurmountable odds!

And by we, I mean ALL of the artists, writers, and Blizzard team members who have worked their butts off over the last three years to get these books out the door and into the hands of you wonderful fans. Many thanks goes to Jason Bischoff, Joshua Horst, James Waugh, Micky Neilson, Evelyn Fredericksen, Samwise Didier, Tommy Newcomer, Cameron Dayton and Chris Metzen.

Our goal when we embarked on this journey was to create the most well written and visually compelling stories possible. *World of Warcraft* is no longer just a game for fans; it's a way of life. Fans play the game to escape their problems for a few hours, converse with friends, and have the adventure of their cyber-lifetimes. It is my great hope--and wish--that we have achieved that level of escapism with our *World of Warcraft* manga.

But, equally important, now that the job has ended and the publishing battlefield is finally still...

Now I finally have time to play the game.

- Troy Lewter
Editor

CREATOR BIOS

RICHARD A. KNAAK

Richard A. Knaak is the New York Times and USA Today bestselling fantasy author of 40 novels and over a dozen short stories, including most recently the national bestseller, *World of Warcraft: Stormrage.* He is also well known for such favorites as *The Legend of Huma* & *The Minotaur Wars* for Dragonlance, the *War of the Ancients* trilogy for *Warcraft,* and his own *Dragonrealm* series. In addition to *Warcraft: The Sunwell Trilogy,* he is the author of five short stories featured in *Warcraft: Legends* Volumes 1-5. He also recently released *The Gargoyle King,* the third in his *Ogre Titans* saga for Dragonlance and *Legends of the Dragonrealm,* which combines the first three novels of his world. To find out more about Richard's projects, visit his website at www.richardaknaak.com.

JAE-HWAN KIM

Born in 1971 in Korea, Jae-Hwan Kim's best-known manga works include *Rainbow, Combat Metal HeMoSoo* and *King of Hell,* a series published by TOKYOPOP. Along with being the creator of *War Angels* for TOKYOPOP, Jae-Hwan is the artist for *Warcraft: The Sunwell Trilogy,* as well as Richard Knaak's four-part short story featured in *Warcraft: Legends* Volumes 1-4.

NEXUS POINT Q & A

A journey that began with the smash-hit *The Sunwell Trilogy* has finally come to a close with *Dragons of Outland: Nexus Point*, concluding the epic journey undertaken by Jorad and Tyri several years ago. In honor of this momentous occasion, we thought it would be fantastic to get scribe supreme Richard Knaak's final thoughts on this manga series!

Tell us about the origin of *The Sunwell Trilogy.* Was this a story that you pitched? Or did you and Blizzard craft the story together?

I was asked to write a manga, with the understanding that they also wanted to introduce manga fans to the world. That required creating a story that first brought the reader some knowledge of the world, then leading them into a storyline more intricate. When I was told about the Sunwell and the fact that Blizzard wanted to resurrect it, I came up with the idea of Anveena. Blizzard liked the concept, asked for my initial synopsis, and then we worked together to craft the final storyline. Always someone who enjoys dragons, I wanted to use one as the main character and since blue dragons are drawn to magic and Blizzard wanted to highlight them, Kalecgos was crafted. After that, the other characters fell into place and the trilogy was born.

Jorad Mace and Tyri have become very prominent figures in *Warcraft* lore. What was the inspiration for these two unforgettable characters?

With Jorad Mace, it was my interest in the paladins in the game. I've always admired the best traits of that type of character, as witnessed in my novel, *The Legend of Huma*. I wanted one who had lived through troubles and so had lost his arrogance, but not his integrity. Jorad quickly became one of my favorites. As for Tyri, I wanted a strong female character that contrasted to the "innocent" one of Anveena and who also had interest in the male lead, Kalecgos. Tyri was also more brash, enabling me to throw her into situations and combat where the others might hesitate.

At times, there seems to be a little bit of romantic tension between Jorad and Tyri. Do you see their story as a kind of romance? Are they soul mates of some sort?

There is a bond between them, a closeness in part because of both being somewhat outcast among their own kind, but it's doubtful that it'll ever be more than a tension. Still, who knows? That's up to Blizzard in the end.

Both Jorad and Tyri have become NPCs in the *World of Warcraft* game! How did you react to their inclusion in the game world? And did you offer to write any on their in-game dialog? ;)

I love that they're in the game! It's fantastic whenever one of my creations becomes a part of Azeroth! It gives them a sort of immortality.

I'd have liked to write some of the dialogue, but I leave that in the hands of the fine folks at Blizz.

Your scripts are very well researched. I know you play WoW, but what other sources do you draw from?

In addition to playing, I'm constantly in contact with the publishing lead and the folks in Lore. Azeroth is a big world and with all going on in it, it's always good to have their help.

Let's talk about dragons! Clearly, you have an affinity for them--as evidenced by *The Sunwell Trilogy*, the two *Dragons of Outland* manga and the *Mage* class-based manga that you also wrote. What do you personally find so appealing about these beasts?

They are to me, along with wizards, the epitome of magic and fantasy. They are powerful, fantastic creatures with so many variations these days. They add an epic feel to any story in which they are part.

Is it going to be difficult leaving Jorad and Tyri behind? If their story continued, where would you take them? What else would you want to explore with these two?

It's rough to leave them where they are. I'd like to explore what happens next, such as how she'll guide the new nether dragons, what trials she and Jorad will face, and who might try to interfere with what Tyri's trying to do. Maybe some day. ☺

Thanks for creating such a memorable manga series, Richard! Do you have any final words you'd like to say about working on such an epic storytelling endeavor?

It always a pleasure to come back to Azeroth and with the mangas, I've been able to see the story come to life in a whole new way. I'm happy so many people enjoyed the tales!

YOU'LL RIDE DOWN WITH THE MARINES. HERE'S YOUR GEAR.
LAGDAMEN CONTROLS THE MOEBIUS REACTORS.
YOU WON'T BE ABLE TO POWER YOUR CLOAKING SYSTEMS.

THIS BE SO FINE!
WHEN YOU GET EXCITED, YOUR ACCENT COMES BACK.
I BE EXCITED!

I MEAN-- I *AM* EXCITED.
THIS BE *REAL* GHOST GEAR!
THERE ARE STILL A FEW POCKETS OF ZERG....
NO PROBLEM.
I'LL BE HAPPY TO SHOW THEM WHAT A *C-10* CAN DO!

THIS IS NOT A *GAME!*
ALL OF YOU, PAY ATTENTION!
THE QUEEN OF BLADES DOESN'T CARE HOW MANY ZERG HAVE TO DIE TO GET TO YOU.

TEAM RED SHOULD HANDLE SURVEILLANCE. WE KICKED YOUR BUTTS ON THE LAST EXERCISE.
KATH IS A BETTER SHOT THAN YOU ARE...
OH, YEAH? ASK LIO HOW THAT TURNED OUT!
LISTEN UP! WE GOTTA BE TEAM PURPLE NOW. WORK TOGETHER.
FOR WHAT? SHE WAS JUST TRYING TO SCARE US.
JUST LET ME GET A COUPLE OF ZERG IN MY SIGHTS--
AND YOU'LL WET YOUR PANTS SO FAST....!

THIS ARGUMENT IS OVER!
WE FOLLOW THE PLAN!

SCANNING COORDINATES 38 MARK 200, ONE HUNDRED TWELVE METERS...
ZZT
ZZT
MOVE OUT!

I WISH WE COULD CLOAK.

STAR TRUCK, THIS IS CHARLIE-TWO.
WE ARE ONSITE AND MOVING.

COPY THAT.
YOU'VE GOT HOSTILES MOVING AT ELEVEN O'CLOCK, 80 METERS.

CHARLIE 1
CHARLIE 2

WE STILL HAVEN'T HEARD FROM LAGDAMEN OR NOVA.
THEY SHOULDN'T HAVE BEEN SO CLOSE TO GROUND ZERO.

THE ELECTROMAGNETIC PULSE COULD HAVE DESTROYED THEIR ELECTRONICS.
OR THEY GOT TOO CLOSE TO THE FIRE.

THEY'LL RENDEZVOUS WITH THE MARINES.
IF THEY'RE STILL ALIVE.

CHARLIE-
ONE.
REPORT.

THERE'S A
LOT OF ZERG
SURROUNDING
THE BUNKER.
WE'RE
MOVING
IN NOW.

I'M PICKING
UP TARGETS
AT FOUR
O'CLOCK.
A LOT OF
THEM. TEN
MINUTES
OUT.

WHERE
ARE
THEY ALL
COMING
FROM?
WIDENING
THE SCAN...

CHARLIE-TWO. REPORT.

WE'RE ABOUT TO ENGAGE!

HOLY FEKK!!
THERE'S ANOTHER CLUSTER OF HATCHERIES!
AT THE EDGE OF OUR SCANNING RANGE!
BIGGER THAN THE FIRST! ON THE FAR SIDE OF MANDIBLE CANYON!!

BOTH SQUADS!! LINK UP AT THE DROP ZONE!
YOU'VE GOT SIX MINUTES!!

SKREEEEEEEE
SKREEEEEEEEEE
SLURCH
SPCOSH
BLAMM
BLAMM
BLAMM

COME ON!
WE CAN HELP!
GOT ANOTHER ONE!
THIS BE CRAZY!!

THERE'S TOO MANY!!
TOSH, WE SHOULD CLOAK NOW...!!

WE CAN'T CLOAK. LAGDAMEN ISN'T HERE...
BUT I AM.

THE MOEBIUS REACTORS WANT TO POWER UP.
THEY WANT TO.
I'LL TELL THEM IT'S ALL RIGHT!

WAY TO GO, LIO!!
VWEEM
FRESH BUG JUICE, ANYONE?!
LET'S GO GET 'EM!!

WHOA! I'M OUT OF POWER...!
BWOOP
I NEVER SHOULD HAVE AGREED TO THIS...!
OUR TURN, ZERG!!

CLEAR!
BESS!
ROCKHAM!
CLEAR!
YOU TWO! YOU'RE SAFE NOW!
BWOOP
DECLOAKING NOW.
SAVE POWER.

NOVA?! BUT YOU'RE DEAD...!
YOU'RE ALIVE?!
YES! AND NOW I'M A GHOST!
WE CAME TO RESCUE YOU!
WE CAME TO RESCUE YOU!
THANK YOU!
TH- THANK YOU...

READY FOR DUSTOFF.

MORGAN! ANTONIA!
DID ANYONE ELSE GET OUT?!
NO, WE'RE IT.
NOVA! YOU'RE SAFE!
AND THE REST OF THE TEAM?!
ALL GOOD!
NO INJURIES AT ALL?
I SHOULD HAVE KNOWN...
LIO CLOAKED US.

SKREEEEEEE
OH, FEKK!!
GOTCHA!
ZOOM X 10
SLPOORCH
Read the rest in StarCraft: Ghost Academy volume 3!